AMAZING ORIGAMI

Origami on the Move

Catherine Ard

Gareth Stevens
PUBLISHING

Please visit our website, www.garethstevens.com. For a free color catalog of all our high-quality books, call toll free 1-800-542-2595 or fax 1-877-542-2596.

Library of Congress Cataloging-in-Publication Data
Ard, Catherine.
Origami on the move / by Catherine Ard.
p. cm. — (Amazing origami)
Includes index.
ISBN 978-1-4824-2270-2 (pbk.)
ISBN 978-1-4824-2271-9 (6-pack)
ISBN 978-1-4824-2202-3 (library binding)
1. Origami — Juvenile literature. 2. Transportation in art — Juvenile literature. I. Title.
TT870.A73 2015
736.982—d23

First Edition

Published in 2015 by
Gareth Stevens Publishing
111 East 14th Street, Suite 349
New York, NY 10003

Copyright © 2015 Arcturus Publishing

Models and photography: Michael Wiles
Text: Catherine Ard
Design: Emma Randall and Belinda Webster
Editors: Joe Harris
Vehicle photography: Shutterstock

All rights reserved. No part of this book may be reproduced in any form without permission in writing from the publisher, except by a reviewer.

Printed in the United States of America

CPSIA compliance information: Batch CW15GS: For further information contact
Gareth Stevens, New York, New York at 1-800-542-2595.

Contents

Basic folds

Origami has been popular in Japan for hundreds of years and is now loved all around the world. You can make great models with just one sheet of paper... and this book shows you how!

The paper used in origami is thin but strong, so that it can be folded many times. It is usually colored on one side. Alternatively, you can use ordinary scrap paper, but make sure it's not too thick.

Origami models often share the same folds and basic designs. This introduction explains some of the folds that you will need for the projects in this book. When making the models, follow the key below to find out what the lines and arrows mean. And always crease well!

KEY

valley fold - - - - - - - - - - - - - - -

mountain fold ....

step fold (mountain and valley fold next to each other)

direction to move paper

push ▼

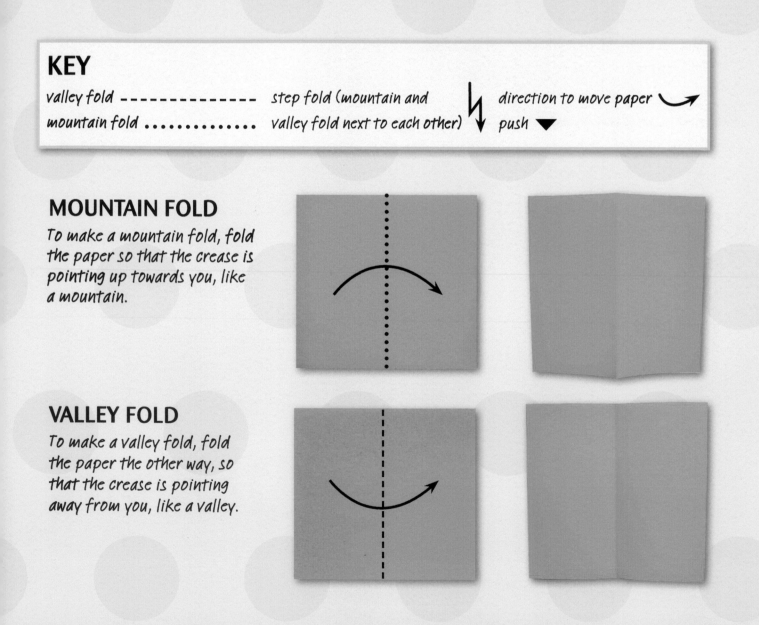

MOUNTAIN FOLD

To make a mountain fold, fold the paper so that the crease is pointing up towards you, like a mountain.

VALLEY FOLD

To make a valley fold, fold the paper the other way, so that the crease is pointing away from you, like a valley.

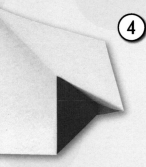

INSIDE REVERSE FOLD

An inside reverse fold is useful if you want to make a nose or a tail, or if you want to flatten off the shape of another part of an origami model.

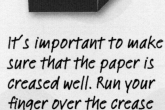

1 Practice by first folding a piece of paper diagonally in half. Make a valley fold on one point and crease.

2 It's important to make sure that the paper is creased well. Run your finger over the crease two or three times.

3 Unfold and open up the corner slightly. Refold the crease nearest to you into a mountain fold.

Open

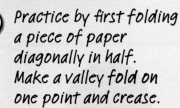

4 Open up the paper a little more and then tuck the tip of the point inside. Close the paper. This is the view from the underside of the paper.

5 Flatten the paper. You now have an inside reverse fold.

OUTSIDE REVERSE FOLD

An outside reverse fold is useful if you want to make a head, beak, or foot, or another part of your model that sticks out.

1 Practice by first folding a piece of paper diagonally in half. Make a valley fold on one point and crease.

2 It's important to make sure that the paper is creased well. Run your finger over the crease two or three times.

3 Unfold and open up the corner slightly. Refold the crease farthest away from you into a valley fold.

Open

4 Open up the paper a little more and start to turn the corner inside out. Then close the paper when the fold begins to turn.

5 You now have an outside reverse fold. You can either flatten the paper or leave it rounded out.

Car

Easy

There are over a billion cars beeping, bumping and motoring along busy roads all around the world! Make a cool car of your own with a few speedy folds.

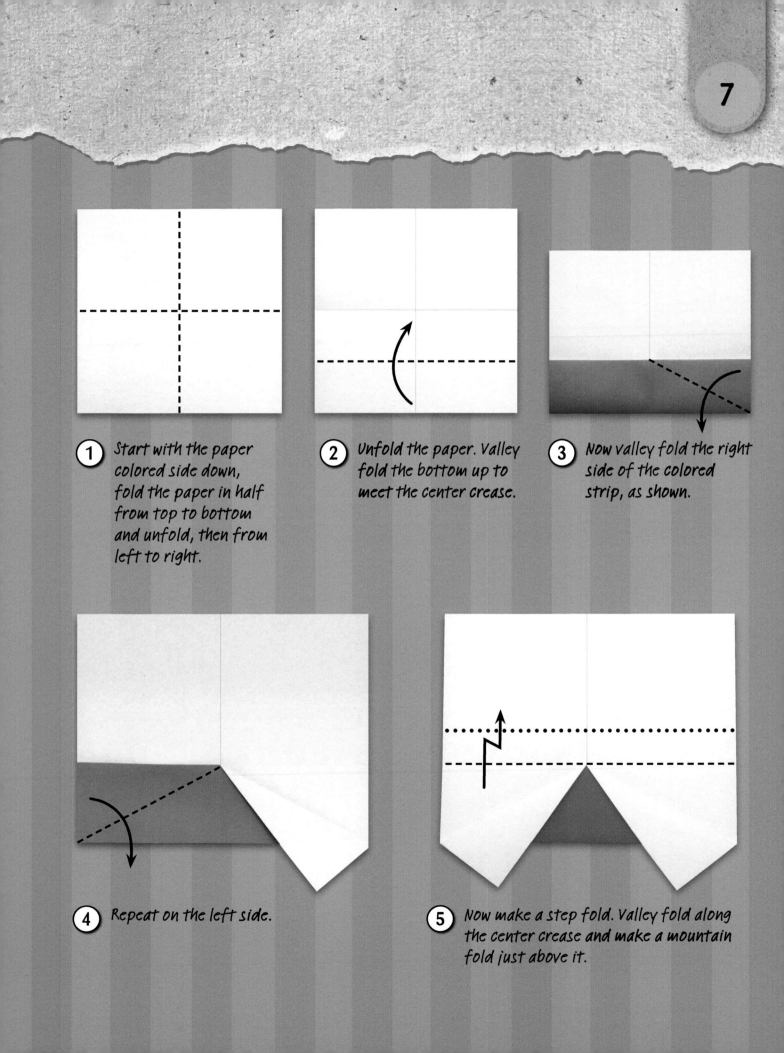

1. Start with the paper colored side down, fold the paper in half from top to bottom and unfold, then from left to right.

2. Unfold the paper. Valley fold the bottom up to meet the center crease.

3. Now valley fold the right side of the colored strip, as shown.

4. Repeat on the left side.

5. Now make a step fold. Valley fold along the center crease and make a mountain fold just above it.

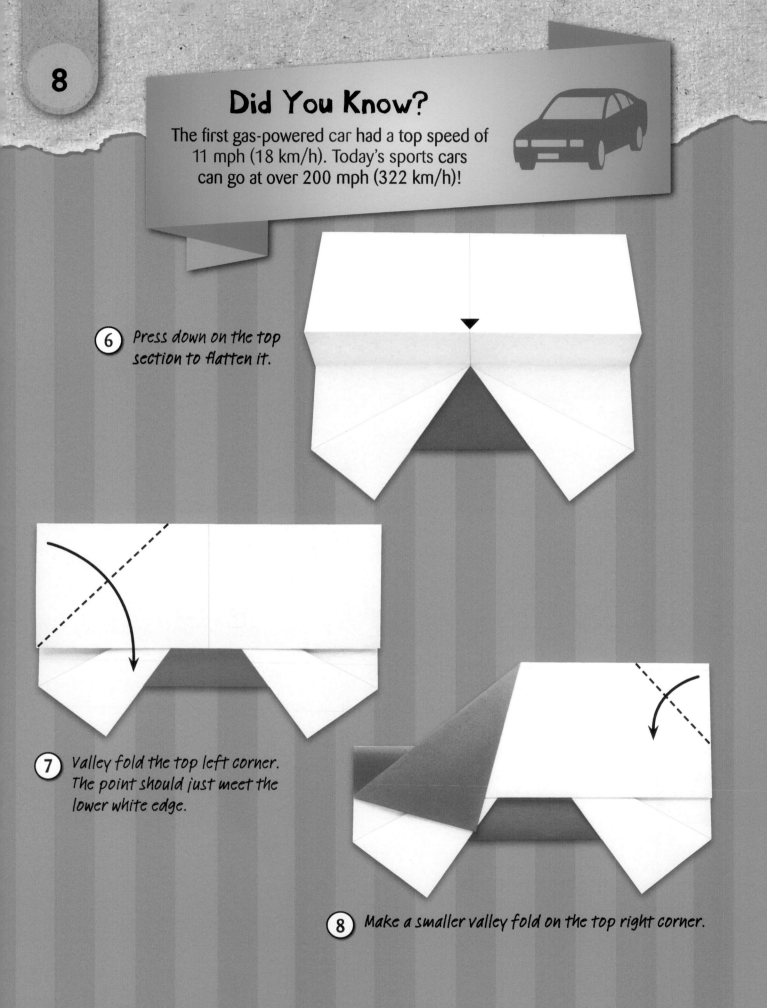

Did You Know?

The first gas-powered car had a top speed of 11 mph (18 km/h). Today's sports cars can go at over 200 mph (322 km/h)!

(6) Press down on the top section to flatten it.

(7) Valley fold the top left corner. The point should just meet the lower white edge.

(8) Make a smaller valley fold on the top right corner.

9 Fold in the tips of the bottom points to shape the wheels.

10 Turn the model over.

11 Draw a door handle and a window to complete your car. You could draw the driver at the wheel, too!

Truck

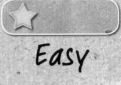

Huge road trucks rumble along for hundreds of miles, carrying goods to their destination. Fold this truck in a matter of minutes, ready to make its first trip.

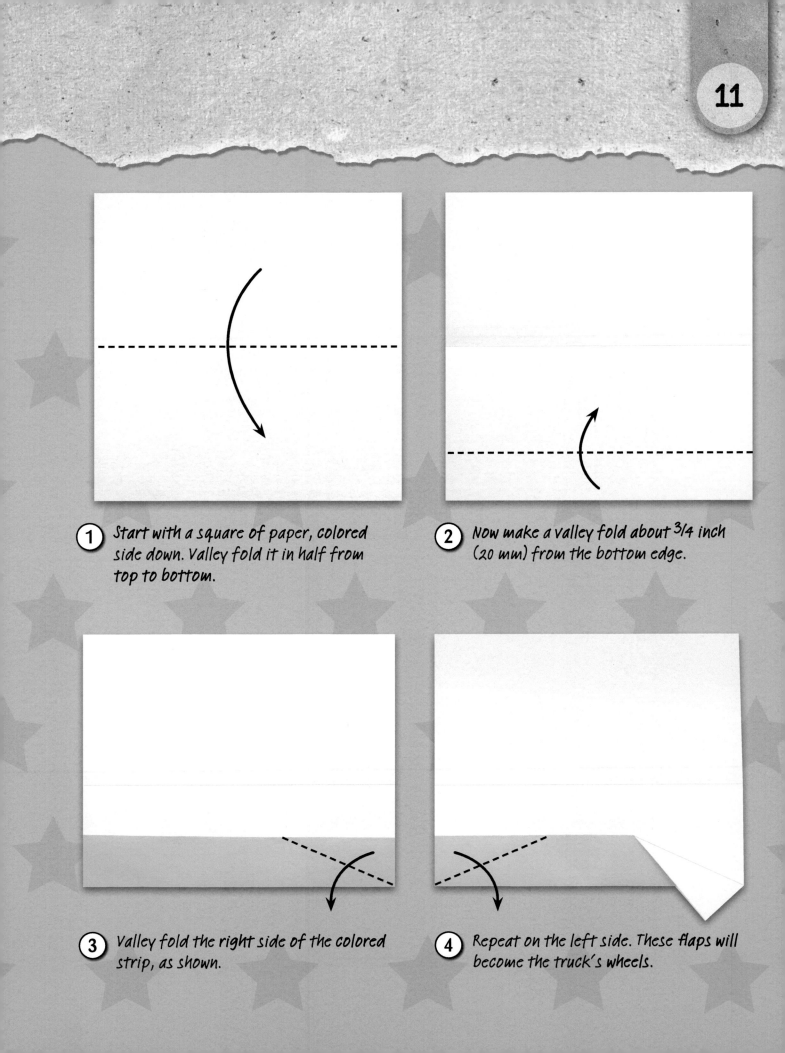

1. Start with a square of paper, colored side down. Valley fold it in half from top to bottom.

2. Now make a valley fold about 3/4 inch (20 mm) from the bottom edge.

3. Valley fold the right side of the colored strip, as shown.

4. Repeat on the left side. These flaps will become the truck's wheels.

5 Turn the paper over.

6 Valley fold the top around 3/4 inch (20 mm) above the center crease.

7 Valley fold the right corner of the flap so that the edge lines up with the top.

Did You Know?

Long-distance truck drivers can be on the road for many days. There is sometimes a cozy bunk bed in the cab for them to sleep in.

8 Valley fold the top right corner. Line up the point with the fold you made in step 7. This is the cab.

9 Finally, mountain fold the tips of the bottom points to shape the wheels.

10 Your truck is ready to hit the road. What is it carrying? Draw a cool design on the side of the truck!

Bus

Buses carry people across towns and cities, taking them to offices, shops, and parks – and then back home again. Ding, ding! It's time to go and fold your own!

1. Start with a square of paper, colored side down. Valley fold it in half from top to bottom, then unfold.

2. Valley fold the paper about ¾ inch (20 mm) from the top edge.

3. Now valley fold the bottom in the same way.

4. Valley fold the bottom right corner as shown.

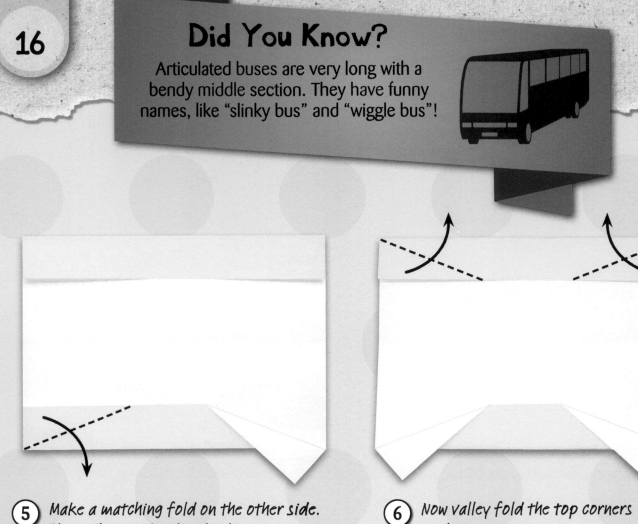

Did You Know?
Articulated buses are very long with a bendy middle section. They have funny names, like "slinky bus" and "wiggle bus"!

(5) Make a matching fold on the other side. These flaps make the wheels.

(6) Now valley fold the top corners in the same way.

(7) Fold over the tips of all four points.

(8) Valley fold the paper in half from top to bottom.

9 Valley fold the top corners and unfold again.

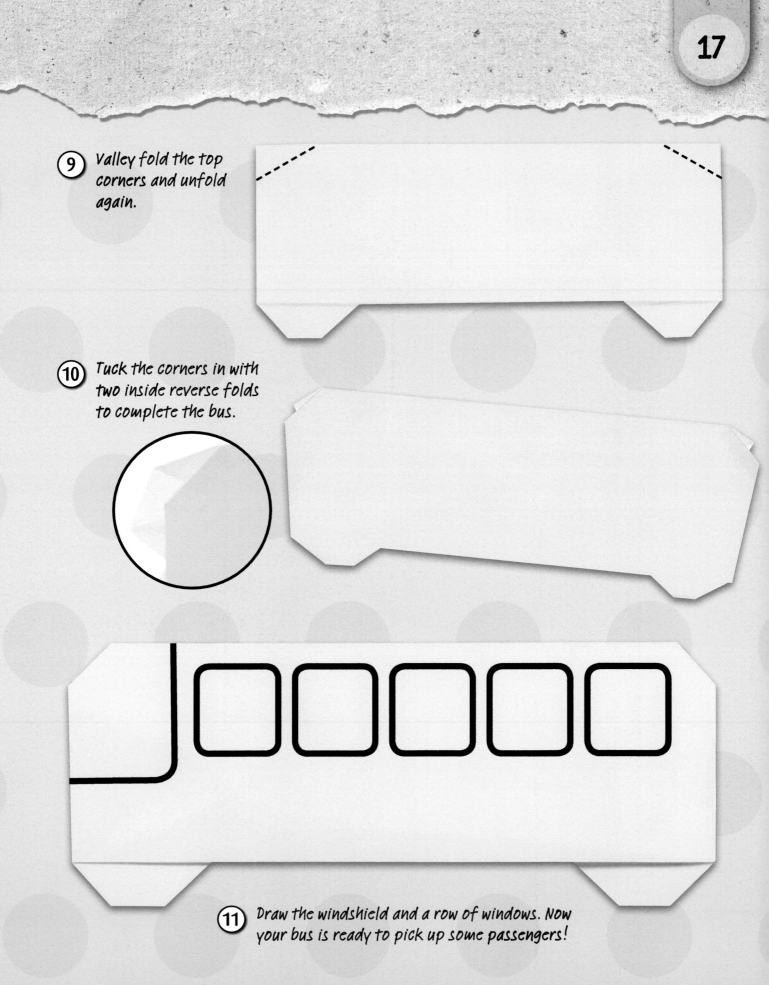

10 Tuck the corners in with two inside reverse folds to complete the bus.

11 Draw the windshield and a row of windows. Now your bus is ready to pick up some passengers!

Train

Trains rattle along the rails, carrying passengers to stations near and far. Some trains are powered by electricity and some have diesel engines.

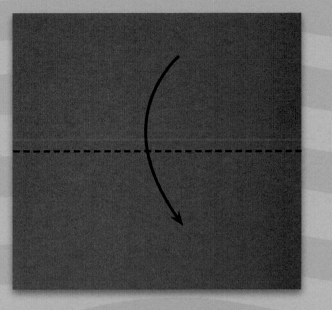

1 Start with a square of paper, colored side up. Valley fold it in half from top to bottom, then unfold.

2 Valley fold the paper about ¾ inch (20 mm) from the top edge.

3 Now mountain fold the paper along the center crease so that the bottom folds behind the top.

4 Mountain fold the underneath layer, making sure the edges line up at the top.

Did You Know?

Some trains don't have wheels.
Maglev trains use strong magnets to
lift them up and drive them forwards.

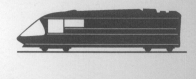

5 Turn the paper so the white strip is at the bottom. Valley fold the top left corner.

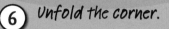

6 Unfold the corner.

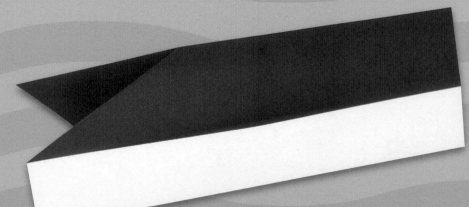

7 Make an inside reverse fold, tucking the corner in to create the pointed front of the train.

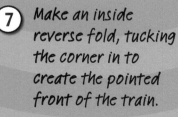

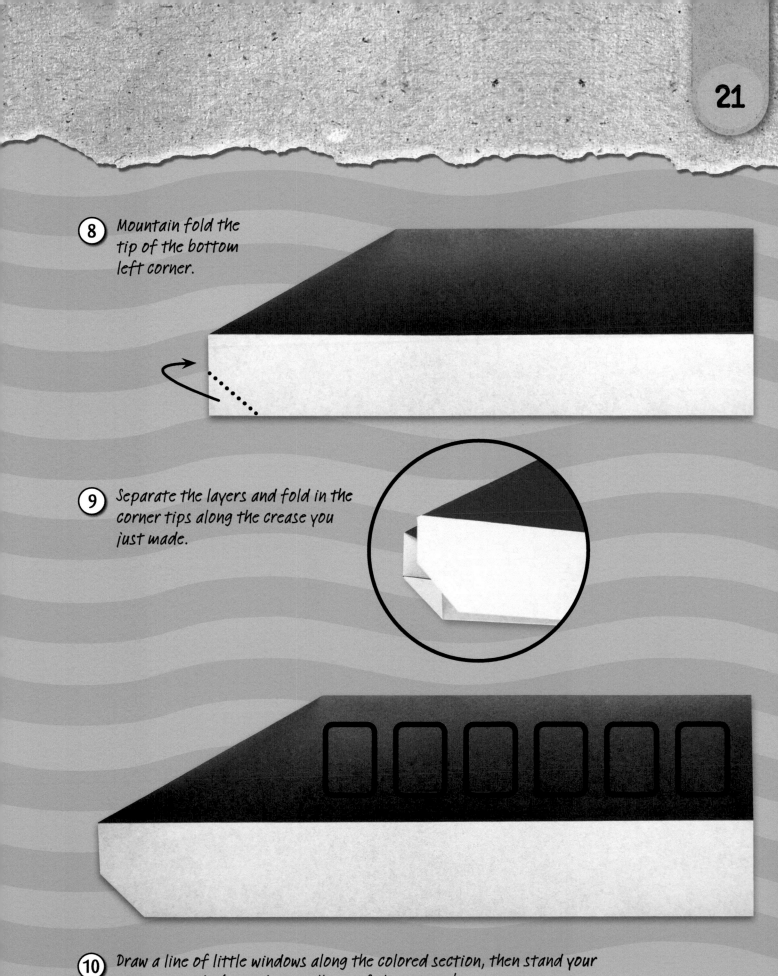

8 Mountain fold the tip of the bottom left corner.

9 Separate the layers and fold in the corner tips along the crease you just made.

10 Draw a line of little windows along the colored section, then stand your train up and it's ready to pull out of the station!

Ship

Medium

Ships are made to sail across seas and oceans. They ferry people, cars, and cargo through calm seas and stormy waters, to ports in countries around the world.

1 With the colored side up and one point towards you, valley fold the paper in half from top to bottom and unfold.

2 Valley fold the top corner to meet the center crease.

3 Valley fold the flap about ¹/₂ inch (15 mm) from the top edge.

4 Now fold down the tip of the point. This will become the ship's funnel.

5 Valley fold the paper in half from left to right.

6 Now make an outside reverse fold. Begin with a diagonal valley fold across the bottom third of the paper.

7 Open up the paper. It should look like this.

8 Push in the sides and turn the corner inside out to make the colorful hull.

Did You Know?

When you are on board a ship or boat facing the front, the right side is known as "starboard" and the left side is known as "port."

9. Crease firmly along the colored edges and your ship should stand up on its own.

10. Draw three round portholes along the upper section. Anchors aweigh, your ship is ready to sail!

Canoe

Long before there were cars, boats, and trains, many people used paddle power to get around. Follow these steps to fold a paper canoe that actually floats!

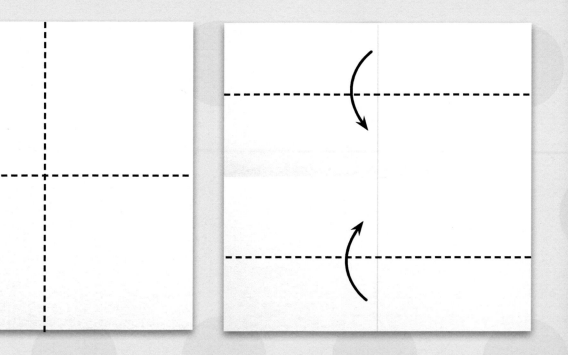

1. Colored side down, valley fold the paper in half from top to bottom and unfold, then from left to right and unfold.

2. Valley fold the top and bottom edges to meet the center crease.

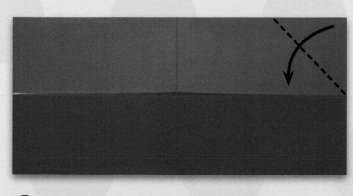

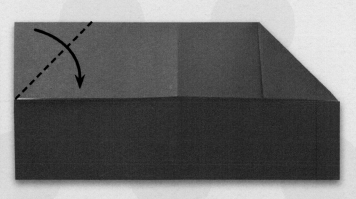

3. Valley fold the top right corner so that the point meets the center crease.

4. Do the same on the other side.

5. Now make matching folds on the bottom corners.

6. Make a valley fold from the center of the top edge to the right point.

7. Make a matching fold on the left side.

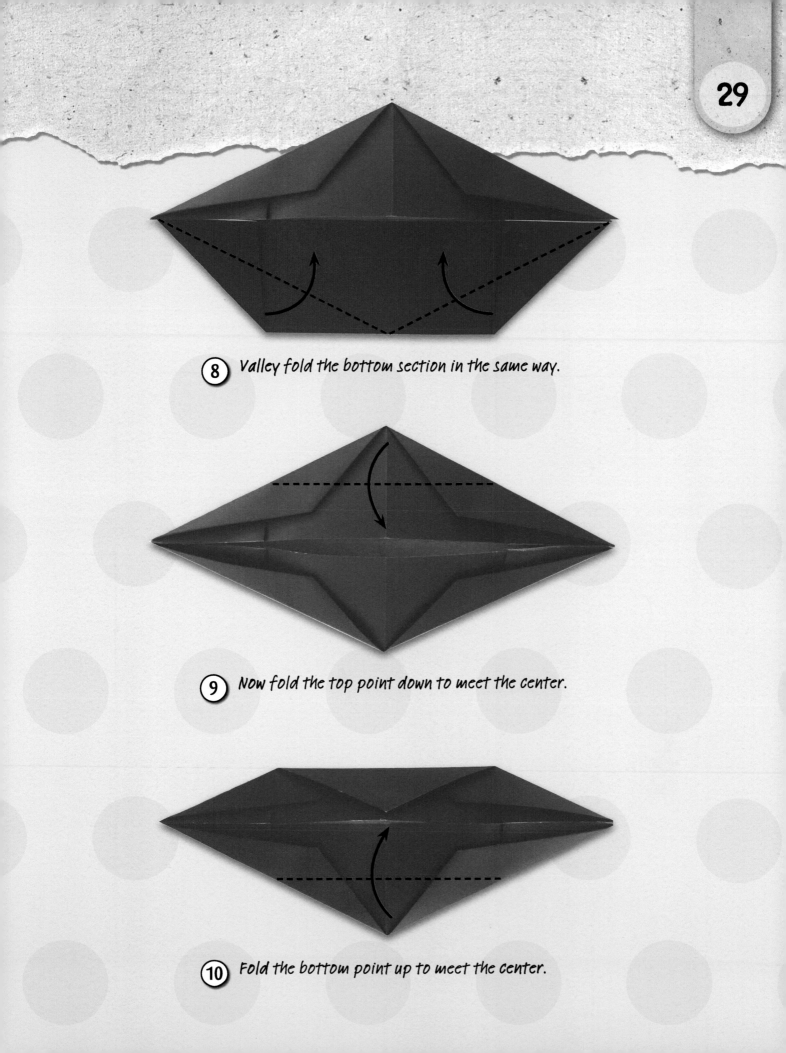

8. Valley fold the bottom section in the same way.

9. Now fold the top point down to meet the center.

10. Fold the bottom point up to meet the center.

Did You Know?

Some of the first canoes were made from big tree trunks. The inside was dug out to make the hole to sit in.

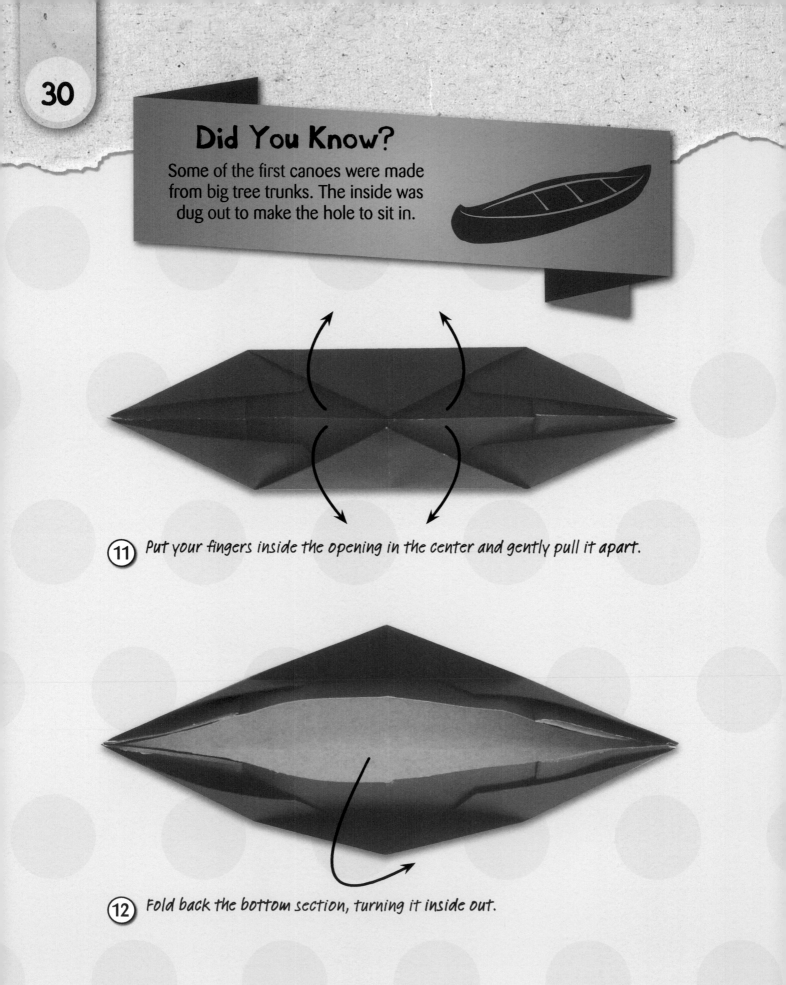

(11) Put your fingers inside the opening in the center and gently pull it apart.

(12) Fold back the bottom section, turning it inside out.

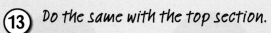

(13) Do the same with the top section.

(14) Turn the canoe the right way up to see the color on the inside and the white on the outside.

(15) Your origami canoe is ready to take to the water. Put it in a pond or stream, or fill a bath or bowl with water. Your model should float!

Glossary

articulated A vehicle that is made up of two or more parts that bend where they are joined.

billion A thousand million. The number is written as 1,000,000,000.

cab The separate front part of a vehicle where the driver sits.

cargo The things that are carried by a ship, aircraft or other large vehicle.

crease A line in a piece of paper made by folding.

destination The place where someone is going, or where something is being sent.

diesel A type of oil used as fuel for vehicles.

funnel A metal chimney for smoke or steam to escape.

maglev Short for "magnetic levitation" – a system in which trains glide above a track.

mountain fold An origami step where a piece of paper is folded so that the crease is pointing upwards, like a mountain.

step fold A mountain fold and valley fold next to each other.

valley fold An origami step where a piece of paper is folded so that the crease is pointing downwards, like a valley.

Further Reading

Akass, Susan. *My First Origami Book*. Cico Kidz, 2011.

Biddle, Steve & Megumi Biddle. *Paper Capers*. Dover Publications, 2014.

Ono, Mari & Hiroaki Takai. *Dinogami*. Cico Books, 2012.

Robinson, Nick & Susan Behar. *Origami XOXO*. Ivy Press, 2012.

Index